Of Life and Love

Jan Rothschein

Published by Jan Rothschein, 2023.

OF LIFE AND LOVE

First edition. January 29, 2023.

ISBN: 979-8215051580

Written by Jan Rothschein.

Table of Contents

OF LIFE

AND LOVE

Jan Rothschein - Of Life and Love.

INTRODUCTION

So how would I start this off, well by not by saying anything too corny I hope, this book serves as an older sister to my first publication called the "The Semicolon" whereas instead of seven parts this book takes the minimalist approach of only being split into two parts – Love and Life – 2 virtues of men that basically cannot exist without each other, let us face it- You need to love someone or something to develop a passion, and passion in my opinion is what gets people going through their daily lives and to go through your day is to live and that explains the symbiosis of love and life.

This symbiosis is the answer as to why many poems feel similar, even connected at times since you will experience same motives while loving, as you would by living.

This about as sums my introduction, and I shall let trademark phrase of "I hope you have as much fun reading this as I did have writing this." Guide you the ever-confusing number hell that is my table of contents on the next page.

Jan Rothschein

Of Life and Love- A Footnote

As two wires in a box
as a dog and a fox
as a cow and an ox
as a sister and a brother
coexist for each other
as a husband and a wife
go together love and life
a dynamic which lay eternal
experiences remain nocturnal
and as you live you discover
secrets you like to uncover
Many live for the ones they love
many love even those they should hate
many live questioning the lord above
many love those not seen as great.
Many live even through dark times
love sometimes beats many crimes
acting okay through life
for some is the answer
many neglect their wife
for them love's a dancer
many see love as a cancer
many live life as a romancer
yet many live looking for a fix
because loving got them stuck in a mix
mix of emotion
resembling an ocean
an ocean so deep
who knows what may creep
om the bottom of this water.
But why do we even bother?
Many strive to get better

while others write love letters
many live with being rejected
many are forever connected
hand in hand, glove in glove
same as then life and love.

OF LIFE - 1

Looking outside
free of fright
there may not be clear weather
but I feel like I'm doing better
it feels like forever
since I've had it all together
but I'm finally able to read books
finally, not breaking down cause my looks
finally living life on full throttle
finally, not relying on the bottle
pushed my own rock up the steep hill
no longer do I worry about other people
this fresh air almost feels like I'm free
of wanting to be under a car or on a tree
finally, I get a chance to unwind
finally have time to calm my mind.
Tell younger me that we did good
tell him we don't feel chained by food
we're living a life we were deserving
instead of worrying about every serving
tell younger me we do what we want
even though people still think we're savant
even though we never learnt to dance
tell younger me we have confidence
even though we feel bad if we boast
tell younger me now we can post
post anything anywhere
say anything without care
tell young me we got rid of every leech
he needs to know infinity has been reached
no one knows how It came to be
but I wish to tell younger me We're free.

Was it the media? Was it the habits?
No one knows what killed all the sadness
no one knows what saved me from madness
Was it that I stopped being lazy?
Was that the thing stopping me from going crazy?
Was it that I started playing games?
Was it that I stopped taking blame?
I don't know what got me motivated
suddenly happy to rise out of bed
don't know which way my life rotated
but I am forever glad.

OF LOVE - 1

hearing people flexing
about their so called "sexing"
makes me shake to my toes
cause I've never come close
never have I held hands
but God knows I want to
don't need that many friends
I just need a one to
to believe in my goals
to reply to my calls
to try and understand
that I am not the man
not the man that I once were
thanks to some people treating me like air
I believed I need to change
ended up even more strange.
As I look around the land that's hard to measure
it seems that people only seek pleasure
seeking it in sex
some wanting to be someone's ex
some wanting to be called a whore
but I do not want nothing more
nothing more than to be kissed
to know if I'll go I'll be missed
to know that I don't have to worry
about my love saying sorry
over being under the influence
giving others the devils dance
I want something pure like a rose seed that's emerging
I want something worth all those years being a virgin
yet I'm scared of women
due to my inexperience

all that talk about sinning
when I can barely dance.

OF LIFE - 2

To the pair of eyes
constantly locked at the floor
serving as a disguise
posing like an open door
when the ears are blocked with music
there's only one entrance so use it
eyes which basically beg for help
eyes compared to a sea or two
eyes that beg and beg for you
eyes looking like fresh ice
with the innocence of mice
eyes resembling meadows
who tend to hide in Shadows
eyes which remind me of canyon soil
probably saw bullets recoil
eyes of many shapes and sizes
like Shakespeare's drama
eyes full of surprises
eyes disciplines by trauma
eyes of a lion
or human being
no matter the kind
they all are gifted with seeing.
Seeing signs
sings which aren't nice
those belong to a life so weary
I see iceberg eyes get teary
I see tears smudge makeup lines
like opening a stranger's mind
suddenly I see their issues
their "I love you" and their "I miss you"
suddenly I can see

see their life as if they were me
see the way they face their fears
all the ways they cry their tears.
Tears that wish they weren't there
wishing they were blown by air
wishing they were wiped by hair
wishing that somebody cared
tears that fall so slow they're bored
tears don't get why they're ignored
The light of those beacons glows
oh my god how I love those
sadly, there's things no one shows
due to them those eyes will one day close
I'll forever dread the day where I'm stripped from this sight
I'll forever dread the day when an angel will loss a fight
what am trying to say is that what I dread
is a day where those eyes lay in the casket dead.

OF LOVE - 2

You asked me why I feel blue
I said I can't really tell
when in reality it's you
who's the reason I go through hell
you're so perfect its troubling
all my image issues doubling
we'd look outlandish together
that's why my feelings never matter
that's why I watch what I say
watch every joke
overthinking immensely
over each syllable I spoke
cause I know damn well
every joke I tell
that that joke could be the last
turn you from present to past.
You don't know my hobbies
and I wish you never will
cause what makes me stand out in lobbies
is just being mentally ill
I am never especially good
I read I'm dumb, I lift I'm weak
I write, I make typos, I cook, I ruin food
compared to me, you're so unique
never can I be truly myself around you
sometimes I regret the day that I found you
you make me scared of every move I make
you make me scared of every breath I take
around you I walk on eggshells
while you just stress my cells
stress my brain stress my heart
make me want to tear myself apart

rip out every organ
just to never be seen by you again.
To you I'm a puppet with no string
a club with no dancers
so every night I think
think up a question with no answers
how did I even gain your interest?
was it your pity or my humour?
cause you look like you're from Pinterest
and I don't even look human

OF LIFE - 3

O road, my road lead me on
o road, my road lead me on
lead me where I feel like home
lead me where I have my throne
lead me on your trail of mystery
lend me a piece of history
lend me a little spark
to shine for me when it's dark
lend me a little dove
make me fill him up with love
lend me a little post
to raise up when I feel lost
lend me a little lamp
to make me feel like a champ
lend me a little light
make me rid of all my fright.
O road, my road oh give me power
make me stand tall like a tower
make me walk as long as I feel my face
make me worship all your grace
make me watch the cars which ruin you
cry over the holes they blew in you
strong sign of civilization.
O road, dear road please lead the nation
show us all a giant favour
point us towards our saviour
for some of it is not a thing
it's not a person with a ring
it's not a man that cannot sing
it's not a chain that cannot bling
for some it's hidden, in difficult code
for me it's just you, my lovely road.

OF LOVE - 3

When did love stop being forever?
When did it become talking shit,
and doing "it"?
I look at that and think its whatever
the world spins and I spin along
need to adapt, need to be strong
but why are looks the only thing to matter?
I think to myself as I get fatter
will me and her ever be together?
Will I dread the fact she has someone better?
Everywhere I look
I can't compete
I'm like an unfinished book
all is so incomplete
and all the boys I'm around
by women they're surrounded
a good style they have found
and their body well rounded
yet why am I the clown,
who'll forever wear the frown?
I'm the one left lonely
daily I am feeling down
feeling like I want to drown
cause I don't have a one and only.
Feel myself getting lost in vanity
chasing perfection, losing sanity
just to be liked for a little while
I'd do it all for a perfect smile
I'd change my soul for people to love me
I'd starve for months just to be lovely.

OF LIFE - 4

like a leaf of bay
unwanted in soup
I feel pushed away
from ever group
When did I get so alone?
Feeling like a dog without a bone
Did these people leave?
Did I make them?
The promises I believed
Did they break them?
Do I deserve to feel lost all the time,
feel punished in every moment?
Is heaven punishing a crime?
A crime I didn't commit
every public place I step in
I feel the approach of danger
constantly overstepping
being treated like a stranger
was it the others or was it me,
making me an alien of society?
When did my life lose all good feelings?
When did it become just staring at the ceiling?
Why do I struggle to show emotion?
When the thoughts in my head could fill an ocean
Why do I lack will to live?
Why do I lack fucks to give?
s life after death better?
I think to myself writing a goodbye letter
word after word I keep writing
to make my way out exciting
cause the only way that people care
is if you're no longer there

the moment when your life ends
is when you tell apart fakes from friends.
Cause it's always the biggest actors
the role they played was the big homie
who wouldn't pass a lie detector
if asked on how well they know me
might be lonely, might be sad
and sometimes this feeling bothers
but this the life I'd rather have
than being falsely loved by others.

OF LOVE - 4

In a moment of weak essence
I still think about your presence
have you thought about me back?
When they left you feeling wrecked
as I tried to get your emotion
and believe me I tried
you just dreamt of jumping into an ocean
with all your limbs tied
your sunshine turned into rain
as you dreamt of getting rid of pain
to me that day just felt unreal
when you described the pain you feel
I tried to be your support even when you didn't care
now I don't even know if you are still there
I don't know how worse or better have you gotten
I just hope that you never have forgotten
forgotten the night we spent with a smile
got to say right now it's been a while
hope you didn't stoop low.
I hope you sometimes message
if you want to see me you know
you can find me where the mess is.
The memories hurt
you said you hope to be his wife
sadly, tides have turned
now I'm praying you're alive
praying you carried on
that you still laugh, draw and sing
everyday just feels wrong
where I don't hear your ding.

Since you've broken up with him
you've been questioning your position
hope you're still trying the gym
hope you fulfilled your condition
hope you didn't write a note
that I didn't get to read
hope you still slay in your coat
hope your throat did never bleed.
I don't regret a nice thing
I ever said to you
I hope some did bring
a bit of happiness to you
now with this I want to tell
you I don't want you in hell
wish I could be of some help
now we both just hate ourselves
wish I was back there by your side
make sure there's no chance of suicide
well, you sent me away with pride
so, with shame I ran to hide
now I will always regret
being that weak
I should've kept my thoughts a secret
not let you see me as freak
we don't talk anymore
guess it's been a year
every time I'm feeling bored
I waste time hoping you're still here.

OF LIFE - 5

The year is slowly coming to an end
I've died trying to follow every trend
died finding someone I won't repulse or offend
every time I gained a friend
I've come to lose two more
there was no way to defend
us not having topics anymore
spend the year without a kiss
yet there's still people to miss
I was to see so much blood
it feels like the year was just a red flood
made more rhymes than I made dimes
still, I'm yet to commit any crimes.
The year came fast,
nothing did last
I can't describe this with precision
but if I had to find one word
I think that the whole world
would agree it's "decisions"
be they good, be they bad
we've made a lot of them this year
we were happy, then we were sad
some were always filled with fear.
yet this year I was to realise
I am nothing but a bag of lies
lies I tell others,
lies I tell my brother
lies that have no one to bother
lies that contradict one another
I lie to myself that I feel good
while I keep avoiding food
I make myself seem like someone else

while I feel like seven hells.
The year comes to an end
and I'm thinking damn
there are letters to send
to the man I think I am
maybe the reason this year felt gritty
was me spending it faking an identity.

OF LOVE - 5

I've told you I loved myself yesterday
must have been April fool's
went ahead skipped dinner today
cause I'm tired of feeling like a tool
a tool to people to look and giggle
in every roast battle I'm stuck in the middle
tool to be the butt of all jokes that go far
tool to be told its less worth than a car
tired of my life playing s quiet melody
so, I've realised it had to be my body
I started losing mental clarity
shushing my health for popularity
tried to be lovable, tried to be slim
cause skinny and loved are often synonyms
tried to be perfect for every gaze
yet now I hate myself most of my days.
In a quest for perfection
I've gained fear of my reflection
fear of the scale
as in my room I wail
as I aimlessly try with no success
to recover but it's a slow process
cause every time I see myself look good in a suit
I start feeling like no breakfast is good
passing on nutrients till my skeleton's rotting
I hate to see all this pain amount to nothing.

OF LIFE - 6

Wish that some of you were still alive
to see your words and letters thrive
to see your greatest work survive
to see the impact on human life
wish some of you see the sun
with our new technology
wished some never grabbed the gun
or messed with psychology
now with all this off my chest
there are some people to address.
oh, in the ancient times
countries of no laws
full of crimes
many flaws
a lot of mines
eagle's claws
fresh pepper grinds
these lands birthed great minds
from Plato through Homer to Aurelius
their wisdom great, their life Mysterious
no matter the climate no matter the weather
these minds kept writing to make futures better
many died of illness many fell in wars
I want them to know their work is now in stores.

Shakespeare, I wish you could hear
all the people using your rhyme
wish I could talk to you ear to ear
make an exclamation about time
wish I could hear you say who you hated
what do you think of the language you created .

Verlaine, Rimbaud, Wilde
you would have to hide
nowadays you'd glow with pride
sounds like a dream, am I right?
Nowadays you're free to love
whoever tries to touch your glove
wish you would see your statues made of bronze
nowadays you'd be icons.
And to Pushkin oh your fate was cruel
I believe you wouldn't duel
if you chilled with all the antics
still, I enjoy your romantics
I hope that you saw the change
in love that you might consider strange
and to the other Russian tragics
just know I see your work as magic.
Freud, Adler, Jung please hold tight
hate to say it but you're right
it'd certainly buff your groove
if you saw modern people prove
everything you said was true
and that's why I adore you
cause nowadays all the trends
somehow stem from our parents.
Czech interwar authors
I'd love to tell
you that he's dead
his moustache's in hell
nowadays people listen and learn
admire the works that they used to burn
Often, I think of suicide
but there's things that keep my mind off her
what helps all those feelings hide
are words of yours,
My dear authors philosophers.

I wish you knew the life you make us live
your words be the gift you give
every time I'm feeling low
these words of yours is what helps me grow
And Kafka I'd like to just ask
which nation is credited to the task
of housing an author so great
sadly, for his own art he had housed hate
you'd be wondering like "what the hell?"
You predicted the world like Orwell
for your generation you were out of luck
now many people want to be a bug
Bukowski, I Wish you saw
life in Brno with no law
fun, loud, dangerously gory
like if straight out of your story
wish you could see the guys
who sometimes read your books
wish you could see the sights
the dystopian looks
wish you could see the vocal gold
that some of your quotes still hold
but sadly, you never will
I just wish you were never Ill.
Cobain, wish you could see your music
and the way that people use it
wish you could see Dave's new band
wish you could see the latest trends
cause even though they say it's not true
deep down they all dress like you
wish you could see your children grow
and scream at the crowd at your show
sadly, your case is hard to figure
wish I knew who pulled the trigger.

Respect to all dead greats
but I must show
the one who for me weights
in the front row
the one who made hair raise
with stories of a crow
I express all my praise
to Edgar Allan Poe.
Oh, what to say
it feels like theft
so many paved the way
so many left
be their death quick, be it slow
be they from whatever nation
I just want them all to know
they were the biggest inspiration
and there still people to remembered
from January to December
there bands missing a member
there are letters that miss a sender
just know that,
In any case this world gets rotten
yet don't matter how old it's gotten
your works never will be forgotten.

OF LOVE - 6

As I strut down the avenue
see all the cars were made for two
Olden lovers walk shoe to shoe
look eye to eye
and I wonder why.
As I look at the house next door
see a happy family of four
love from the cellar to the corridor
who could've asked for more
though I'm shook to my core.
As I see them holding hands in gloves
true unrequited love
I ask the god above
when will he send a dove
when will he make the shove
and make me feel loved.
As I walk home cold turn on the tv
happy pairs are all that I see
they're together holding tightly
their energy so carefree
and their movements careless
has me feeling jealous.
As I look at the sky
to ask God why
19 years and no ex
looking for someone to rely
on while they look for sex
I try to have my feelings on their wall
but no one cares, no not at all
I'm looking for someone to make
me feel like I want to wake
wake up not thinking I'm a mistake

make every day smell like fresh bake.
As I realise, I always am the third wheel
While I just need someone to make me feel
that happiness is still very real
need someone to make egoistic
but that shit's just not realistic
cause as modern media changed love's tone
it led to some people being left alone
golden and cold hearts left to rot
wishing they belonged to someone they're not.

OF LIFE - 7

As I wake up in my bed
thinking about words I never wish I said
questioning why the sheets are wet
pondering what breakfast is to be had
my morning starts with a stretch
and a shower so nothing does scratch
present nicely even though no one will care
sometimes I even brush my hair
there is never procrastination
in my morning quest for validation.
in the bus I hide my face
in the city I try to take no space
I try not to be recognized
as I hide behind my coat of lies
lies I tell to make me better
such as hiding my head in sweaters
telling myself I have it all together
and that's it is going to get better
in my school I rarely talk
it's just sit and walk and sit and walk
try to get some education
on my quest for validation.
After school I exercise
to shrink some extra size
maybe it's just time I waste
trying to for once like my waist
sometimes I do it to feel good
about overeating food
sometimes to feel satisfaction
sometimes to give my life traction
sometimes to just feel some tension
try give my bad life an extension

trying to have a body of godlike creation
is just another part of my quest for validation.

I come home and feel so cold
still can't find a hand to hold
write poetry about time of old
or the rendition of a heart of gold
starve my mind of every rhyme
that came to me in today's time
write about something unreal
or just about how I feel
write about a bad day
or something that's deep
then put the pen away
proceed to go to sleep
hope my craft will one day be an inspiration
for now it's just another way of getting validation.

OF LOVE - 7

You

I don't know what to say
every time you talk
you just take my breath away
I bet
you feel like real good song
every time we talk
I just know that nothing can go wrong.

You

I feel that you're very strong
it feels crazy how
you always get along
with everyone
or at least everyone you want
you're the type to make them run
if they're messing with your aunts.

You

be it September or may
but every time you walk
it's like you're on a runway.

You

feel like a real good book
every time you step out
man, it's worth a look

You

I don't know what it took
maybe you casted a hex
cause you got us all on a hook
and maybe it is your smile
just to see it live
some would probably walk a mile.

You

have an interesting style
but getting ready probably
takes you a little while.

You

walks around like you don't care
I always think gee golly
when I see your luscious hair
your friends say
talking with you is super fun
it's like you have a positivity gun
you feel like a good ray of sun
every person who knows you
has automatically won.

You

can't do no wrong
everywhere you're number one
you can slay it in a fur
and you can slay it in a bun
they assume you're kind of quiet
but I wish that you'll shake off
what's not making your future bright.

You

I see that you're very educated
lots of class
and I bet your room's well decorated
you're just super dedicated
to everything you do
and I hope that you will make it
I am not finished about dedication
I just really hope you know
you're my muse and inspiration.

OF LIFE - 8

You say I'm ill
and I should get help
but just when will
you hear what I want to tell
tell you about me and the way I was raised
and how it led to me hating my face.
I'm obsessed with one thing
and that is my look
I'm doing anything
to look like a man from a book
cause they paint men ideally
be they big or small
while I focus to eat freely
as my hand hits the wall
my other obsession often has me spitting
and that is my desire, desire to fit in
I'm willing to change everything I know
I'll pretend like I know your favourite movie and show
even pretend we have the same favourite colour
just to make the world feel smaller
to fit in I'd do it all
id rise and then again fall.
thirdly I obsess with love
I always ask the one above
why do I always get ignored
by the ones I always adored
is it the way I look? Dress? Smell?
Oh, to feel perfect id walk through hell
safe to say those obsessions
are hindering my healing progression
committing a spree crime
robbing me of my free time.

Overshadowing
what I do for fun and where
sometimes I think
if I'm still the man I once were
thinking of the past
has me very stressed
but I want to go back
to before I was ill and obsessed
obsessed with others and the human will
obsessed with love and myself
want everyone to stop calling me ill
want them to stop saying I need help.

OF LOVE - 8

You were home to me
and you left me feeling homeless
with you I knew where home could be
now I don't know where home is.
Should've never told you how I feel
should've convinced myself you're not real
should've never shown you my emotions
knowing you'd just throw them in the ocean
ocean in your mind where you harness useless information
we had nice future, though it was only my imagination
you told me to never change
stay who I am
but how can I not consider it strange, coming from someone who chose to
treat me like a lamb.
Like a lamb to the slaughter
you tied me to a chain
went through hell and high water
just to find out your name
to find out who you are
behind your disguise
went very far
and got caught up in your lies
nothing you said was ever meant
I felt like you set up a tent
a tent in the middle of my brain
where every lie you tell drills me with pain.
Oh, what a fool I was to believe
when you said you would never leave
cause while you were such a pretty crier
you turned out to be an ugly liar.

So, I long to forget your face
move on forward leave no trace
but the lies you said to me
are the thing that set me free
your words are what I truly miss
as I fall back into the abyss.

OF LIFE - 9

When God gave away ordeals
I must have been Abu Dhabi
when God gave away ordeals
I must have showed up late
when God gave away ordeals
he just gave me a body
when God gave away ordeals
and it's still something I hate.
you know what I'd find neat
Others than feeling like I'm enough?
Not thinking of what I eat
and how many steps to burn it off
I did all the things to see myself thinner
yet all my efforts came in vain
as I see myself in the mirror
and my heart is filled with pain
and I have tried everything
even wishing on the magic rings
it's like nothing works to me
it's like this was all meant to be.
why can I live?
Seeing every body as fine
then I cannot give
the same praise to mine
everyone has strengths and everyone has flaws
sometimes I chewed gum until it hurt my jaw
and still my face is rounding
I'm despised by my surroundings
seems they all want to avoid me
cause I don't have a good body
I'm the butt of every joke
just a poor skinny fat bloke

who tried to change with unfinished hikes
instead, he became the one no one likes.

35

OF LOVE - 9

Apple of my eye
I don't even know why
every time you walk by
I feel a little shy
maybe it's your exterior
that makes me feel inferior
maybe it's the glance
that makes me feel I have no chance
I am yet to know your hobbies
but I feel like we'd share a lot
I hope that you at least know me
I'm spending nights playing "likes me, likes me not?"
Sometimes I hope that you notice my style
maybe you'll know that I'm worth your while
but you don't ever bother to give me a look
not even a slither of time
we're like a poem in the book
but we do not rhyme.
I'm running out of time
I'm someone you wish you never knew
I should give up on chasing you
but I hate you with someone new
if you are ever near the forest
there is someone you may see
tell him what's wrong and be honest
cause that someone might be me
I just want to know
before we get lost in the mix
I just want to know
Did I lack something I could fix?
Was the way I lived that wrong?
Did you hate my every move?

Did you just wish to remove?
Remove me from your sight
make my messages not ring
cause for you I might not be right
but to me you were everything
it's hard to forget your mistakes
and there had been a few
got to ignore headaches and heartaches
for the centre of my view.

OF LIFE - 10

It fills me with glee
when I see women in groups of three
cause in men it causes stress
one is always treated like less
one is the butt of every joke
the target of every prank
the neck of the fatter one they choke
the saggy chest of his they spank.
Male groups, I believe are pressed
to always come out pretty
to always be well dressed
girls just have personality
and they're happy with that
be they seen as fat
be they seen as flat
they don't seem to mind
they're content with what they find
what amazes them in this world
makes them act like little girls
Oh, how I cherish these moments
how I sometimes wish to be a woman
to have friends that don't act strange
when your face begins to change
men promise to ride or die
then leave you wondering why
what did you do to make them leave
all the time they're faker than a weave
empty promises they lay
cause a pain that won't go away
meanwhile when I see a few girls gather
no matter what they stick together
there could be arguments, longer than a pink Floyd song

but somehow someway the feminine bond holds strong.

Younger me wouldn't understand
how hard it is nowadays for a man to make a friend
we all got tweaked expectations
all got different inspirations
remember when we talked about action heroes
and the plans they were plotting
now we are just a couple zeroes
socialising by rotting
we talk about nothing
and everything at once
we know we would be something
if we just found something fun

OF LOVE - 10

I still keep the messages you sent
they live in my head, they don't pay rent
and I thought you were going to stay
sadly, we had a deadline day
I imagine you in all the places
see the spot where your face is
meant to be
wish you could see what you're meant to see
I just wish it didn't hurt
I know you still owe me my shirt
We know there's much music to be heard.
Every time I see a bird
a bird that's so blue
a singing little bird
always reminds me of you
every red rose
reminds me of your lips
the lips that felt like time froze
the lips I always wished to kiss
the green of the meadow
reminds me of your eye
as in smothered eye shadow
it told me the final lie.
I miss our little walks
our silly little talks
but I don't know who to blame
for things not staying the same
was it me or you that lost?
Now that our bonds at permafrost
now we both lack a hand to hold
two hopeful hearts turned cold
now I'll be on track

waiting on the dark side of the moon
if you're willing to come back
please come visit me soon.

OF LIFE - 11

I wish I was you
so I wouldn't stress over my shoes
stress over a sip of mountain dew
stress over what I say and do
I wish I was more socially active
maybe that could make me be more attractive
calm my need to be overreactive.
Wish I fit in without trying
through every convo I'm flying
at home I feel like dying
dying lacking a real friend
dying wounded, no one to tend
tend to the wound that is my loneliness
and the need to overdress as means of success
success of hiding what I had seen as a flaw
success of the skin I carry at law
I wish it was brighter
I wish it was clearer
I wish my skin was tighter
wish there was never a mirror.
Sometimes I wish for you not to have eyes
so I can't see them as I hear beautiful lies
sometimes I wish I wasn't just a disguise
just a costume you use to make yourself feel nice
I wish that people would get me
to speak freely they should let me
my mind would get clear
and I would appreciate greatly
if someone could hear
what I have been up to lately.
Am I finally perceived,
as more than dirty dishes

have I finally achieved,
some of my wishes?
Sadly, I have not
in my solitude I rot.
Sometimes I wish there was something to rate me
tell me the reason why people hate me
sometimes I wish there was someone to date me
when I die, I wish that in hell, there is someone to interrogate me
so, I could say wished my parents haven't made me.

OF LOVE - 11

I hate the one you love
because you always put him above
he gets to hold your hand in glove.
He's the one you see as fun
he makes you feel like I should've done.
I hate the eyes outside
from their gaze I cannot hide
it's a punishment I've received
to stay feeling perceived
I can't stand people's gazes
can't stand going through phases
I hate saying fake phrases
like "it's going to get better"
"it's just ketchup on my sweater"
and "yeah we still talk together ".
Know I wouldn't be there
without their interference
but I don't think I care
when I say I hate my parents
for how weak they make me feel
for teaching wrong ways of what's real
for always pressing me down
and forcing me to hide my frown
to hide who I am
questioning if I am a man
just because of them.
I hate myself because I overcommit
and when things I fail, I want to vomit
I hate myself because I don't know what's good
and when things fail, I binge on food
I don't know when to stop
with everything I do

that's why I always hate my top
my hat, my pants my shoes.

I hate the way my hair looks on my head
I hate that I once made myself hate bread
I hate everyone and everything
due to this I'll never be given a wedding ring
I hate isolation
yet hate every friend
I hate my odd imagination
it made me hate who I am
an image I want to be
a perfect version of me by me
is what I'll sadly never see

OF LIFE - 12

Professional family disappointment
target of generational hate
I find myself missing appointments
and staying up late
my room is a mess
and my mind full of stress
I keep spending on temporary happiness
then doubting if I'm even worth having a penis.
Since I know my mom cries
but she won't show it
she's tired of all my lies
but I shall never know it
with dad I find common ground
but she cries when I'm not around
cause we can never agree
not even over my choice
of clothes, of friend of a degree
feels like she hates to hear my voice
to my brother I rarely speak
and I watch week by week
as our relationship deteriorates
I go to work, he goes on dates
or maybe he hangs out with friends
I don't know, he doesn't share plans
we both know we are keeping secrets
we don't keep memories they'll turn to regrets
it's been a few months since we showed compassion
to each other
maybe a victim of my depression
was my tie with my brother
traded our games for obsession
with an unrequited lover.

I never can see
even from the highest tower
a sight of me
ever stooping lower
than I stooped back then when
I was cutting ties
with each and every friend
calling them out on fake lies
if I knew back then
that I was plotting on my own demise
I'd take my pen
and write all the lovely lines
to those that I knew wouldn't leave me
to those who always believed me
never could I see myself alone cause how
would I lose all that love me?
If only past me could see me now
locked in my room starving to feel lovely.

OF LOVE - 12

you said you like them skinny
so, I chose to starve
seeing it as thinning
with thoughts that I would carve
carve my fat way
thought you'd like me that way.
You said you like when they make music
so, I tried to sing
for money and then use it
to buy you a diamond ring
sadly, I wasn't blessed
with an angelic voice
so, all my "career" I was stressed
made fun of by girls and boys
why was I trying to impress
someone who never saw me as their first choice.
You said you like them smart
so, I'd try writing a book
god I tried so hard
just to make you look
make you look my way
make you think I'm worth your day.
You said you like flowers
so, I picked some for you
it took away all my willpower
when you responded with "Ew"
You said you liked crystals
so, I tried charging mine
while you were changing misters
I was holding back crying.

You said you like them earning
so, I tried to get a job
worked till my body was burning
while you acted like a snob
but every time I came home
you were never there
I was always alone
imagining touching your hair.
You said you like when they smell nice
so, I packed my back and went
down to Miami vice
to find myself a scent
found one for me, it was precise
but it was worth my rent
still made the sacrifice
oh, how weak has my mental been
you and I both know this
even that can't make me noticed
noticed by your grace
instead, I see disgust in your face.
You said you liked them stylish
so, I worked on my style
dressed like billie Eilish
and it worked for a while
sadly, there was no amount of money
to save myself from feeling funny
cause all the cash I spent on clothes
yet you don't want to let me close
let me close, let me hear
hear your anger, hear your fear
since you said you liked spirituality
I tried understanding empathy
you said that you like them romantic
so, I tried practicing kissing
just to hear about your antics

all the dudes that you've been missing.
You said you like their jaws sharp
I took the bait like a dumb carp
chewed gum until jaws hard
honey that's the worst part.
You said you like when they skate
so, I tried to fit in
but I just filled myself with self-hate
convinced myself that I can't win
I never got the hype
I could've asked you out to dance
I'll never be your type
cause you said you like confidence.
You said you like them unhealthy
so, I started smoking and drinking
yet slowly but stealthy
my health started sinking
so, I started thinking
I asked myself why I do
all of this because of you?
Your words left me with an aching slow heart
a heart that doesn't beat
beat the way it should
but when I thought you and I would meet
I believed that it would
it would come back to its senses
you made me lower my defences
just to make me feel the same
the way they all claim
they claim I should feel like shit
because I have no hand to hold
rotting in a hellish pit
thought you had a heart of gold

When you told me
you like when he goes to the gym
I couldn't see
that you were talking only about him
he who had your heart
right from the start
he'd look at me and smile
laugh at me for staying a while
it won't be a crime
to laugh at a man wasting his time
see when all his plans backtrack
the man knows he was not loved back
never was and never will
that's why he shall remain ill.

OF LIFE - 13

Late night
I try not to fall asleep
instead, I write
every though to ever creep
through my head during the day
each one that was deep
made feel some kind of way
I don't mind the clock
I don't mind the time
my mind as if locked
focuses on only rhymes
is this even real?
Why am I not tired?
Sometimes it feels
as if I've been wired
wired by someone from heaven or hell
blessed with rhymes that I'm excited to tell
as letters pass
the sun starts to rise
like water on grass
the sweat wets my eyes
looking at the shine
through the curtain slits
wondering when it is time
time to call it quits
what started as fun
ended as a chore
luckily a one
that will never bore
no matter where I am
I could be in another nation
in my head I still scram

words and their combinations
with rhymes my brain does juggle
he sees it as a duty
even though the heart does struggle
the brain creates beauty.

As I finally close the paper
containing all my words of sorrow
I can't wait to return later
and do the same Tomorrow

OF LOVE - 13

He slowly entered the room
we talked about MF doom
knew he was from Catholic school
but oh my god he was so cool
a man of his style
I haven't seen in a while
told him "I don't know what to do
be you or be with you"
then I heard his dad yell
saying he'll go to hell
for once making a choice
that he is into boys
his emotional sway
made him feel a bad way
I know this can't be real
can't fight the way I feel
haven't saw him in a while
drowned my sorrow at pubs
then he walked with a smile
saw me at the club.
The smell of his cologne
has me shaking to the bone
I see him touching my thighs
I wish that we'd do something nice
like they did back in Rome
I wish I could take him home
but it just would be wrong
cause what makes a Czech guy worse than a sex offender
getting with someone of the same gender
but he's so lovely it makes me mad
we feel what some people wish they had
every time in with him I feel safe

in his presence I would bathe
he makes me feel soft
in a land sorrow.

Sadly, we got to sleep in a loft
that his parents borrow
there are things I can't tell
I can't tell why I feel like this
I don't want to go to hell
but it might be worth like this
I wish we had more time
wish they didn't see us a crime
wish he didn't have to hide
wish we both could show our pride
wish we'd let our hands hang
out of his quick Mustang
as I feel the speed rise
I enter paradise.
Said "you can read my letter but don't burn it
sit down every word might be worth it
I feel sorry for all the women I tried to flirt with
they might consider this rude
but the person I consider perfect
is a tall-ish dude."
Few days later word got out
that he feels the same
while I was feeling proud
he couldn't handle the shame
couldn't handle the hate
his parents made him face
just because he wasn't straight
he was seen as an alien race
took a toll on his mental it was clear to see

he hated himself for liking me
I hated myself for making him feel
feel like he doesn't deserve to be real
as days went by, I felt he got eaten up by blame
our lowly ship slowly sank
tried to visit him and reignite the flame
on his door I was greeted by bang.
A few days later paramedics found him
in a bathtub with only a gun to surround him
no id and no note on his side
still, they had to call it a suicide
another person died hating his choice
another silence of a hopeful voice.

OF LIFE - 14

What makes you a great poet?
Some say it's the obsession with punk
or the smell of cheap Moët
that will never get you drunk
some people would say no
and act like they know
what makes you a great poet is the ability to show
to show what you feel
to bend what is real
to show your calm rage
to show every stage
every stage of sadness
all the way to joy
portray inertial madness
and things it destroys.
What makes you a poetic creature
is having an outlook on the outside and nature
looking at life while keeping your thoughts lyrical
looking at life awaiting a miracle
writing down every thought and feeling
writing down words that could fill a ceiling
writing about everything to ever exist
still, I don't think what makes a great poet is this.
What makes you a great poet
is looking at life
take chances and don't blow it
like twists of a knife.
What makes a good poet is acting descriptive
giving every occurrence their own perspective
although this sounds rude
I don't think anyone's right
what makes a poet good

is hidden in plain sight.

What makes your poetry great
depends solely on you
depends on how you keep your mind intact
depends on how you see your tongue's impact
depends on how well you watch your words
how well you handle your own curse
depends on your stomps
be they loud or be they gallant
how you handle life's prompts
how you keep your talent
your legacy depends on the way you lived
how did you handle your personal gift
the search for the answer officially ends
what makes you a great poet is just in your hands.

OF LOVE - 14

When I saw you leave
I couldn't believe
I never saw the crack in us
then I watched you turn to dust
all in a matter of a week
all of them feelings felt unique
you told me you had no plans
then I saw you at the dance
ran into you at the gym
just to see you holding hands with him
funny how quickly you've moved on
funny how you managed to prove wrong
prove wrong every one of my doubts
your life went up north, mine went down south
the message of our song was clear
I thought of you ever time I was to hear it
on the radio while I was on the way
to do the job I always will hate
always wondering why, I couldn't wait
why did I have to shower you with hate?
Was feeling like you're lost
never to be found
then when I miss you the most
you decide to come around
decide to come around
with the worst attitude
make my life a roundabout
always talking about some dude
you always come around
like a birthday once a year
always followed by the sound
of my biggest fear

every day that you show up
I wish it was the last
cause it makes me throw up
to feel haunted by the past.
I always feel good
feeling like I know myself
then you come and change my mood
then you come and put me through hell
wish you never would come back
cause every time you tempt me
to feel like you're something I lack
and that makes me feel empty
wish that one day we can meet
and end up on good terms
wish that you would take a seat
and we said goodbye to returns
wish we addressed our issues
and what was always wrong
wish we could stop saying "I miss you"
wish we'd stop being headstrong
wish we could see the way we bonded
as we had both been cursed
wish you never had responded
wish I never texted first.

OF LIFE - 15

Why do I spend money on books
that I'll probably never read?
Spend money on my looks
buying things that I don't need?
Spend money on a scents
that won't get me compliments?
Every one of my vents
dryer than a dish with no condiments
They say that money can buy happiness
well, I do not agree
cause I spent my money on manliness
and I still don't feel free
spent all cash to try and be better
then I end up hating every sweater
hating the way my soles
squeak when they touch the floor
drowning in mountains of clothes
yet still wanting more.
I spend way too much on food
even things I should avoid
but it makes me feel good
and temporarily fits the void
spending money on addictions
put my life in contradictions
spending cash on decorations
though there's no need for celebration
yet my inability to save
has me working like a slave
working a job that I hate
where I always come home late
always come home tired
wishing I was never hired

wishing that I quit
spending money on stupid shit
I won't ever need.
Sooner or later, it's going to hit
That this side of me, full of greed
side of me chasing vanity
starts the descent to insanity
cause in the quest for validation
teens tend to lose concentration
spending to destroy yourself
creates a faster road to hell.

OF LOVE - 15

If you want me to be honest
I still want your heart to be where home is
we might have been bad at the time
but a return is never a crime
and I'm waiting on our spots
will you come? Oh, probably not
I could wait of centuries
while I'm clogged with memories
such as when you were in my house
you had some odd marks on your blouse
like those on the floors
then I was told behind closed doors
"no one will ever love a face like yours"
and I begged heavens on all fours
I was left with no answer the answer was me
told myself I'm going to make you see
see what you lost, but I've lost my mind
lost my friends, my soul, and my smile to a useless grind
I haven't changed, at least not as of late
I'm still the same shell of a man filled with hate
hate for everything, I mean all that I see
cause why does everyone always look better than me?
Often, I go around changing my style
but the happiness lasts only a while
I change my hair
I change my manners
yet no cares
cause none of it matters
nobody cares that they treated you shitty
nobody sees you, unless you're pretty
no one notices me yet it's strange
I look in the mirror thinking of what to change

I must need a doctor to rework my face
maybe I would feel less of a disgrace.

OF LIFE - 16

I see women on the street
acting like feral cats
a desire comes from beneath
a desire to be like that
to live so free of life
to just think of being a wife
to living so without care
not to be so self-aware
as I sit and read my books
I can't help but exchange looks
will all the women passing me
their face bright and full of glee
something about that is a bother
I was raised a man, thanks father
yet sometimes I do not feel
like it is my role for real
sometimes I want to feel gentle
paint a cute eye with a pencil
sometimes I want to feel grace
wear long hair to cover my face
though seeing every man, a sex offender
I would love to change my gender
I would like to walk with pride
walking for the other side
instead, I watch my girly friends
do what their dads would condemn
sometimes I join in and pretend
that I am one of them.

OF LOVE - 16

You told me you value my emotions
then threw them all into the ocean
ocean full of those before me
ocean full of people who bore me
remember when we said
we will fix each other
now we both wish we were death
see one another
as a bother.
Remember when I saw your friend
and we tried to get along
oh, how much did you pretend
that you enjoy my favourite song
all the hours listened together
now I will burn a 2-page letter
2 pages full of rhymes
celebrating the times
we were seeing eye to eye
and I wasn't asking why.
asking why did I believe?
You said that you will never leave
I guess forever lost its meaning
Fuck, I even see you while I'm dreaming
why did you promise you'd care
when I was down, you weren't there
while my life slowly came to resemble hell
you made yours seem like heaven, but with someone else
now you both look at me
and you laugh at what you see
you find me funny like I couldn't be real
Yet I wish that one day, what I felt, you will feel.

OF LIFE - 17

Just like flies to something sweet
lies flock around every street
can't find a place where they won't be
somehow many of them come to me
delude me into believing
all the love I'm receiving
made me feel like I deserve
being more than a reserve
being more than the last shot
being what I can be not
lies often tend to alter
alter what people see
but I do realise after
they really don't like me for me.
People lie to make you stay
lie to hide all the pain
they would cause if they were real
they like to control what you feel
lying it gives people power
a good lie can bloom like a flower
a flower of evil inside the heart of man
that dictates what he can't and can
ill lie to the cured, cured lie to the ill
a good lie could always change a mans will.
But is it good to lie
think of what you do
how many people sometimes cry
just because of you?

Like when you told me that in me you like what you see
then you went for the dude who looked so much different from me
or when I was told that I am special
only to be put under immense pressure
when I was told, I have a social spell
only for years of pure torment and hell
when I was told that they like me for who I am
only to become a butt, of jokes that I don't understand
when I was told, a change will do me good
just to spend years battling with food.
I can shrug of many lies
hide the tears, act tough
but I've come to realize
the biggest lie is that I'm enough.

OF LOVE - 17

Remember us talking
about our dreams
then both of us walking
through different scenes
you don't recognize me
not anymore
and I don't recognize you
that's for sure
I always wanted you
there with me
yet we didn't exactly
care did we
it's so sad to think about
what we stood for
but life's hit a roundabout
put us ashore.
Remember girls and boys
always waiting
now I just see our pool toys
sadly deflating
looking at our spots
is depressing
cause now our happy trots
replaced with stressing
and I saw you round the town
you didn't wave back
you feel like you wear a crown
but it isn't that
do your Pa and Ma still
know my name
walking up our hill
don't feel the same.

Remember when I took my bike
and rode to your place
now I don't know what you look like
you've lost your face.
Remember us talking
bout our dreams
then both of us walking
through different scenes.

OF LIFE - 18

Often, I feel as I've been given a task
to go everywhere wearing a mask
mask of my true self that no can see
a mask that conceals what's really me
a mask that only takes the likable traits
the less desirable are meant to wait
waiting to show in a moment of weakness
as I get home the mask fades with quickness
why have I been conditioned to act like this?
To fake my behaviour just to exist?
To act as if my drink
has been spiked
to do anything
just to feel liked
when have I attained this persuasion
for my peers and their validation?
When I was younger, I wasn't scared
to show myself because no one cared
but oh boy was I wrong
I got treated like shit
cause I wasn't too strong
cause I wasn't fit
cause I wasn't in
cause I wasn't thin
and all of that made my mood crappy
why do this to someone just because he's happy
after that moment I've begun to change
everything about myself that could be seen as strange
began to strip myself from my pride
every "odd" hobby I needed to hide
needed to win every popularity race
so, a transparent mask was put on my face.

But when people aren't here
when no one's around
it gets very clear
I can no longer be found
I cannot truly know
just who I am
cause to everyone I show
a whole different man
every day I try
and switch my disguise
every day I ask why
and look at the skies
why do I have to fake
everything for allies?
Why did you have to make
me lost in my lies?
I'm lying to everyone even myself
one day I'm going to lie my way into hell.

OF LOVE - 18

Read the paper
that said you're doing better now
turned thoughts of me into vapour
got your life together now
while I still sink low
to become something, you will never did know.
Sometimes when I don't feel right
I think about the times you cried
all the tears falling over my actions
cause I lost myself chasing satisfaction
I admit I acted like a jerk
I didn't see the way I've hurt
you but you acted like it's not my fault
picked up the phone whenever I called
the phone rings now, it seems you can't say hello
what are you up to? I want to know.
You've been there all the time
through the times best and worst
it kind of felt like a crime
how you kept putting me first
since I struggled with my identity
it was nice to know I'm someone's priority
but the affection now you never show
where are you? I wish to know
and to the heavens I always yell
things I always wished to tell
tell you ever since we parted
all the hobbies I have started
all my failures and successes
all my pretty little messes
all my efforts to do good
treat someone the way I should

the way you should treat a human
with you,I regret what I was doing.

If I could turn back time, I would return to that day full of snow
make sure you never leave, or at least let me know.

OF LIFE - 19

As the music got loud
and the party got started
aside from every crowd
I have departed
why did I even try talking to the host
he's probably the one who hates me the most
this was meant to be a celebration
though I don't belong in no conversations
the person I talk to the most
sometimes feels like a ghost
I want to branch out, but I can not
so, in the corner I can rot
the quiet pillar with a glass in his hand
kind of wishing he was laid under sand
wearing a nice outfit with no one to notice
he's wondering when the best time to go home is.
Kind of wishing he was home
wishing he could just write a poem
meaningful dreams spin his dome
dreaming of a life somewhere in Rome
new start, new house, new friends
new surroundings, new me, new trends
people on the dancefloor have fun
acting like they're homies
everyone knows everyone
But who the hell does know me?
If I were to fall
would anyone hold me?
However, when I stall
there's always someone to scold me
as I lie to seem tough
I realise I was never enough

Was it even fucking worth it
always trying to be perfect
trying to be pretty, trying to be liked
trying to be smart, never wearing striped
trying to be healthy, trying to be hot
always trying to be someone I'm not
always pretending
that my life isn't ending
as the music gets loud
I wave goodbye to the crowd.

OF LOVE - 19

Beauty beyond imagination
where could we find this sensation
must look to another nation
her smile is the final destination
her kind words
could heal all burns
you can hear sweet songs of birds
everywhere she turns
when your day is at a zero
she could turn you to a hero
and when the clouds out are not calm
she could always keep you warm
and even on days she feels shitty
she can light up the whole city
I don't know a lot about her
but to see her I'd eat soil and dirt
whatever she does she perfect
whatever shell touch is worth it
if your situation isn't the best
with her it can't worsen
kind of scary how fast
she became my favourite person
and her eyes they're oh so pretty
the best possible shade of brown
though it makes me feel a bit shitty
when below them is a frown
cause I understand even angels
can sometimes feel anger
In these times I just don't want to be a stranger
in these times I just want it to be clear
for her, I was, am and will be here.

OF LIFE - 20

It is cold out and snow falls down
lonely trams and empty frowns
people rushing into buses
buses that speed up all their rushes
busses that lead them into malls
malls bordered with see through walls
walls that are met with a gate
a gate which you cross is too late
it's too late now you must buy
something stupid and you don't know why
why do you even celebrate
a birth of a person who's a debate
a debate of their existence
their religion be a sexist stance
stance of the market always goes up
up like the wrapping paper filling every shop
shop workers everywhere filled with stress
stressing everyday yet you feel blessed
blessed from buying something with one use
something with one use that you'll probably lose
something shiny under a plastic tree
a plastic tree that never will see
never see what it's like to be real
to be a real tree, the pain it must feel
as its cut down to celebrate a religion in a house of atheism
cut down for a holiday pushing capitalism
where some children get a lot
some get none
people left in the house to rot
celebrating with a gun
sure, Christmas is a blessing
but who is there to bless

in a shell of a man stressing
struggling with loneliness.

79

OF LOVE - 20

The love of my life
is something I'll never get
but the love for the night
is clutching her cigarette
outside the club
in the smoker's place
she got love
written all over her face
in her hand lay a lighter
god, is she a fighter
men, she keeps on rejecting
insecurities, they are projecting
by the time the night has gone
she knows she will go home with one
one lonely smoker surrounded by voices
one lonely smoker making big choices.
Choices to take the ones doing the least damage
choices to take the ones that won't harm her image
choices to take someone who'll offer them cover
may they be rich or just a great lover
choices to take someone who might treat her right
despite her knowing it's just for one night.
A man who lied and promised forever
in the morning is nowhere to be seen
she takes her pills, she cleans her sweater
and plans to repeat her nightly routine.

OF LIFE - 21

I tell you what you want to hear
watch you smile from ear to ear
say goodbye as we approach the tram
but you don't know that I live in fear
of you finding out what I am
when you're not near
when you find out I play out roles
taking parts of people's souls
to everyone I'm something else
every word rings different bells
like a master of disguise
I'm digging my own grave of lies
cause once there is a time when a man alone is
he will regret his lies, regret not being honest.
I tell you I was there and here
tell you I saw this and that
tell you I see my future clear
tell you I don't think I'm fat
tell you I know my clothes size
tell you I know I have a prize
but it isn't a big surprise
that all of those are little lies.
Little lies to twist the hate
pretend like it's not too late
to change everything about my image
to make myself forget the damage
the damage caused by past tyrants
abused with words or even violence
every word of mine was misused
leaving me full of trust issues.

Now as I watch my old self dying
can't stop this new clown from trying
watch every action of his with fright
does he even know what's right
he built himself a fake palace
where he sips from a made-up chalice
he lies about people, places, shows
becoming the one no one knows
but soon he'll know it does no good
soon he'll know he should've told the truth
when all those lies of his fall apart
when all his friends chose to depart.
Here the clown looks lays, very lonely
wishing he spoke the truth only
wishing he choked on his lies
I know the clown; he was my disguise.

OF LOVE - 21

You asked me why did I disappear
since you finally saw the real me
but see that's the whole problem dear
you should've never clearly
I'm scared of being honest
and if I tell you what's the bother
you leaving will make me the lonest
you'll easily cling onto another.
You never asked me about myself
I always overshared
words built towers from heaven to hell
yet you never cared
despite that if you ever need help
I'll always be there
but you asking about my health
of that I am pretty scared.
When I start being loud
that's when the real me comes out
and I feel you stopping to love me
feeling myself stopping to be lovely
why do I do that, spazz out without asking
just keep attention to me, my traits I am masking
as I try to fit your type
hid parts of my room on skype
tried to hide the way I look
behind the cover of the book.
but as you uncovered my lie
you can't help but wonder why
but I would rather die
than to truly tell you why
for some reason I get scared
by the thought of us together

seems to me like you never cared
not for each one of my letters.
It is clear your memory doesn't work right
since you know nothing about me
yet I remember every night
which was spent wishing you'd live without me.

OF LIFE - 22

Books that are ought
ought to be bought
bought to satisfy my thoughts
thoughts of intellectual thirst
thirst for reading something first
first of a group of smart people
people that scheme something evil
evil we never see
see all beautiful evil lying in poetry
poetry we all read with our eyes
eyes that often struggle to see lies
lies told to us by people that we love
love can turn blind when drawn on a dead dove
doves fly out in the afternoon
afternoon packages arrive soon
soon they'll be opened to reveal books of all kinds
all kinds of books for all kinds of minds
all kinds of minds for all kinds of ideas
ideas of dreams often left at an Ikea
left at an Ikea, dreams often lay broken.
Broken people are often left hoping
hoping to savour all their sorrow
in books that they open
in books that they borrow
drown all their sorrow in fantasy worlds
drown all their sorrow through incredible works
drown all their sorrow in complicated words
what I mean by this is ever since there were letters
humans moved forward- mostly for the better

OF LOVE - 22

Every time I open my eyes
I wish that I'll see you
cause upon many beautiful lies
you're the beautiful truth
I wish you were the sun
so, I could always spin around
every time you text me it's fun
I know there's no time to be down
as you work hard for your goals
I'm here rooting for you watching your story unfold
though i wish that I were part of your story
I'm still here to bathe in your grace and glory
every day I just wish to be near
hear every worry, every fear
hear every giggle, brush every tear
until then I just can't disappear.
You make me thankful that I didn't slice my neck with a knife
you make me thankful to have you in my life
every time I think about you it starts to smell fruity
the fresh smell of citrus accompanies your beauty
every time I think about you during bad weather
the image of you just makes my mood better
every time I think about you trying hard in school
I think to myself like "damn she so cool"
every time I think of any face you make
the image I see cures me of every ache.
There is no way that I'd ever depart
from a girl like you so beautiful, so smart
from a girl like you with such a golden heart
from a girl so pretty, it made me not think of suicide
from a girl so sweet it made me Always want to be by her side.

Believe me, for you I'd do anything
I'd climb, I'd run I'd even sing
I'd go through whatever
no matter how hard the endeavour
I'd go through whatever
just to be at your side forever.

OF LIFE - 23

One day I'll die
as I lay in the casket
And a bird will fly
as I remain masked
No one knows why
And no one will soon care
People would lie
And say they were there
For me before I died
Yet they just offered to share
Share their critique of me
Without asking for a reason
When will those clowns see
I'm approaching my final season.
As I'm losing all that's great
Knowing it's just me, the thing I hate
Want to approach heaven's gate
But I'm aware it is too late
I find it Hard to believe
But if I chose to leave
There's a lot of people who'll miss me
Maybe even wishing they'd kiss me
I'll leave mad at myself for not making history
And turning the fates of those that love me to a mystery
As I fight with all this pain
trying not to go insane
trying not to blow my brain
as I fight to get out
of this hole I fell in
I know I'll make some people proud
I know that one day I'll win
win over my demons

never succumb to their demands
leave the table with a smile
know I won't come back for a while.

89

OF LOVE - 23

Sometimes really does hit
and I realize I act like a piece of shit
not to others, no they shouldn't worry
to my parents, I got to say sorry
sometimes I feel like I don't deserve
the things they do for me
sometimes I wonder how they got the nerve
to approach me calmly
when I'm acting like a bomb
ready to be dropped
spilling oily balm
on a place they just mopped
then saying it's not my fault loud
when my mistakes getting called out.
Why do I refuse to feel guilt
in the house that they have built
trying to declare a throne
over things that I don't own
why don't I appreciate
that what they do for me is great
mom making sure that I ate
instead feels me up with hate
dad warning me about life's danger
makes me feel a bit of anger
why do I treat them like strangers
when they made me the way I am
I want to grip my mood tight and change her
for them I'll be a better man.
Mom and dad are always here
for me and I see that clear
yet why don't I display affection
letting lose our connection

there will be a day our ties rot
where I won't have a hand to hold
I act a fool, I do it a lot.
I will regret it all when they're old
they're there when I'm cold
they're there when I'm hot
they're my mirror's centrefold
still despite that we argue a lot
about what and what not
so, I might not let it show
but I love them more than they know
I adore every second of their care
and I thank God daily that they're there.

OF LIFE - 24

Every time it gets cold as ice
I feel like I get watched by eyes
eyes that move wherever I do
eyes that know a lie and the truth
eyes which don't know who they chose
eyes that will probably never close.
Every time alone at night
I feel like there's something behind
waiting for me just to turn
so, it can stab, bite, burn
these feelings will never lose me
always scared something or someone will try to abuse me.
In my house I'm never alone
scared, staring at my phone
I can hear impending doom
footsteps from an empty room
in my room there's no one there
yet there still sounds to raise hair
sometimes I feel like its taunting
taunting me making me feel haunted.
Alone at night I'm feeling fake
convinced that someone will take
come and take me, using force
every beep a scream in morse
in my mind everyone who's talking
around me plots on gangstalking
I'm the only one to realise
I'm constantly watched by eyes
sometimes I feel like I'm Truman
but the eyes to watch me are not human.

OF LOVE - 24

Carrying the sound of buskers and Accordion
a city whose castles could scare Napoleon
a city where you never can get lost
a city where everyone has a cost
a city with unique spaces and looks
for that we can thank Mr. Fuchs
for others it's bland for locals it's cool
this the city where I suffered through school
there are some places where I had good times
somewhere I also had very bad times
the city which houses the funniest crimes
its unique beauty must be explained in rhymes
Jošt on his horse with all his might
city of unis, our future is bright
beautiful green parks
take care of fresh air
from schools to landmarks
the trams take you anywhere
friendly people are waiting to greet you
though approach with respect
some may want to beat you
never know what to expect
but that's the local magic
sometimes it's all good
sometimes it's all tragic
however, what puts everyone together
is that this city's charming no matter the weather
big towers everywhere symbols of power
it's forever expanding blooms like a flower
skeletal undergrounds coated with mystery
that's just a brief part of this place's rich history
there are many clubs for the people to dance

enjoy the local nightlife experience
every time you're out
you can meet someone you know
strike a quick hangout
join and enjoy Brno.

AUTHOR'S MESSAGE

Well, here it is Dear Reader

We have reached the end of this journey of Life and Love, Emotions were evoked, and Eyebrows were raised, or at least I do hope so, I do thank you for reading this book and I do thank everyone who made sure this comes out. Also I do thank people that weirdly inspired me for many poems, some being great musicians which I will never get the chance to talk with and whose music played loudly as I wrote the words on these papers.

If anyone claims that a poem from here is based on them, it probably is not

With an invite to read my first book "The Semicolon" and to check my name out on the Allpoetry website I bid Farewell.

Also by Jan Rothschein

The Semicolon
The Semicolon
Of Life and Love
Of Life and Love